We Can Clean

by Bonnie Ferraro

Look at the sand.
The sand is
very dirty.
We can not play
on it.

We can help.
We can clean
the sand.

6

Look! The sand is
clean now.
We can use it. We can
play on it now.

Look at the park.
The park is very dirty, too.
We can not play in it.

We can help!
We can clean
the park.

Look! The park
is clean now.
We can use it.
We can play in
the park now.

Look at the lot.
We can clean
the lot!

Comprehension Check

Retell

Complete the Author's Purpose Chart with your class. Then retell what you learned.

Think and Compare

1. What did the author want you to know?

2. Think of someone you helped. What did you do?

3. How can people help keep a beach clean?

16